AN UNCERTAIN HOUR

A Full-Length Play in Two Acts

by
NICHOLAS A. PATRICCA

Dramatic Publishing
Woodstock, Illinois • London, England • Melbourne, Australia

*** NOTICE ***

The amateur and stock acting rights to this work are controlled exclusively by THE DRAMATIC PUBLISHING COMPANY without whose permission in writing no performance of it may be given. Royalty fees are given in our current catalogue and are subject to change without notice. Royalty must be paid every time a play is performed whether or not it is presented for profit and whether or not admission is charged. A play is performed anytime it is acted before an audience. All inquiries concerning amateur and stock rights should be addressed to:

DRAMATIC PUBLISHING
P. O. Box 129, Woodstock, Illinois 60098.

COPYRIGHT LAW GIVES THE AUTHOR OR THE AUTHOR'S AGENT THE EXCLUSIVE RIGHT TO MAKE COPIES. This law provides authors with a fair return for their creative efforts. Authors earn their living from the royalties they receive from book sales and from the performance of their work. Conscientious observance of copyright law is not only ethical, it encourages authors to continue their creative work. This work is fully protected by copyright. No alterations, deletions or substitutions may be made in the work without the prior written consent of the publisher. No part of this work may be reproduced or transmitted in any form or by any means, electronic or mechanical, including photocopy, recording, videotape, film, or any information storage and retrieval system, without permission in writing from the publisher. It may not be performed either by professionals or amateurs without payment of royalty. All rights, including but not limited to the professional, motion picture, radio, television, videotape, foreign language, tabloid, recitation, lecturing, publication, and reading are reserved. *On all programs this notice should appear:*

"Produced by special arrangement with
THE DRAMATIC PUBLISHING COMPANY of Woodstock, Illinois"

©MCMXCV by
NICHOLAS A. PATRICCA

Printed in the United States of America
All Rights Reserved
(AN UNCERTAIN HOUR)

Cover design by Susan Carle

ISBN 0-87129-534-2

For Primo Levi
and for all who participate creatively
and carefully
in the gift of life

Although this play is based on real people and events,
everything in it, including the person of Primo Levi himself,
is a product of my poetry and, therefore,
an activity of my imagination

The writing of this play was supported in part by grants from the Illinois Arts Council, a state agency; from Loyola University of Chicago; and from the National Jewish Theater, Skokie.

Nick Patricca was awarded the Cunningham Prize for Playwriting by The Theatre School of DePaul University, Chicago, for *AN UNCERTAIN HOUR*.

AN UNCERTAIN HOUR

A Full Length Play in Two Acts
For 9 Men and 2 Women*

CHARACTERS

The Principals:
PRIMO LEVI
JEAN
A BOY
A WOMAN

The Ensemble:
KAPO, STEINLAUF
TECHNICIAN 1, TECHNICIAN 2
BUREAUCRAT 1, BUREAUCRAT 2, LORENZO

*The play is constructed in such a way that it can be performed by an ensemble of nine actors. Because it is truly an ensemble piece the advantages of additional actors are obvious and should be determined by the production concept of the director and the material and human resources of the producing company.

Performed with one ten-minute intermission between acts.

TIME: Saturday morning, April 1, 1987. The day before
Palm Sunday. Three days before Passover.
PLACE: Turin, Italy.

SETTING: A simple, spare unit set. The memory-imagination of Primo Levi is the space-time of the play.
SITUATION: The moment before the death of Primo Levi.

AN UNCERTAIN HOUR premiered at Bailiwick Repertory, Chicago, on May 23, 1994 with David Zak, Executive Director; Cecilie D. Keenan, Artistic Associate; Steve Decker, General Manager and featuring:

Primo Levi	Gene Terruso
Jean	Jim Ortlieb
The Woman	Mary C. Beidler
The Boy	Jay Kiecolt-Wahl
Kapo	Steven Waste
Bureaucrat	Jeffrey Fracé
Lorenzo	Andrew Hawkes
Steinlauf	William Hepp
Technician 1	Guy Massey
Technician 2	Natasha Lowe

Understudies:
for Primo Levi—William Hepp
for Jean—Guy Massey
for Technician 1—William Hepp
for The Woman—Susan Thompson

Directed by	David Zak
Assistant Director	Lauren Stevens
Costume Design by	Christine Birt
Lighting Design by	Julio Pedota
Scenic Design by	Brian Traynor
Sound Design by	Joe Cerqua
Production Stage Manager	John Kokum
Assistant Stage Manager	Dawn Marie Galtieri

Preface

Primo Levi was born in Turin, Italy, in 1919, where he trained to be a chemist. His ancestors were Sephardic Jews from Spain who had come to the Piedmont area of Italy in the early 1500s to avoid the Inquisition of Ferdinand and Isabella. They introduced the silk trade into Italy at this time and specialized in making the dyes for which Italian silk is justly famous. Their native language was *Ladino*, a type of Spanish spoken in certain areas of medieval Spain. In Italy, they adapted this tongue to the indigenous *Piemontese* dialect, incorporating into it many Hebrew words, especially words necessary for the dyeing of silk. To this day, the Italian language uses these Hebrew words to describe types and qualities of silk and their colorings.

In September of 1943, Primo Levi joined a unit of partisans in the hills of Piedmont. The group was almost immediately betrayed by an informer and Dr. Levi was arrested by the Italian Fascist Militia. At the moment of his arrest, for reasons totally beyond his imagining, Primo Levi, a completely secular Jew and atheist, declared: I am an Italian citizen of Jewish blood. This fatal declaration caused him to be deported to Auschwitz in February of 1944 where he was imprisoned until his liberation by the Red Army in January of 1945. Because of his training, Dr. Levi was forced to work as a chemist for I.G. Farben Industries in one of their "factories" in the Buna-Monowitz sector of Auschwitz. This "employment" and the extra food given him by an Italian bricklayer helped Primo Levi to survive almost eleven months in this man-made inferno.

When Primo Levi returned to Turin in 1945, he wrote his first book, a memoir of his experience at Auschwitz entitled *If This Be a Man*, in which he tries to "look objectively" at what happened in the death camps, to the oppressors as well as to the victims. Initially, this book was unanimously rejected by the Italian Board of Censors, several members of which were Jewish writers, for being "negative." The book was published in 1947, however, by a small press, and was largely ignored until 1966 when it was re-issued and became a best-seller throughout Europe. In this same year, Jean Amery, also an Auschwitz survivor, published his definitive work *At the Mind's Limits* in which he also attempts to "look objectively" at the death-camp experience. This work so disturbed Primo Levi that he began an eleven year correspondence with Amery in which they debated the nature and meaning of human existence, essentially arguing about whether we humans are worth saving. In 1977, Dr. Levi retired from his position as a manager of a chemical factory in Turin to devote himself full time to his writing. From 1966 on, Primo Levi's reputation as a writer became well established throughout Western Europe. It was not, however, until his death in 1987 that his work was readily available to English readers in the USA. Today, his work is receiving the attention it deserves.

Primo Levi's writings defy categorization because they are truly unique works of art, possessing elements of the Italian Enlightenment's essay tradition, the Italian Renaissance's philosophical poetry tradition as well as elements of our modern "confessional" literature tradition. In all of his writings, Primo Levi is concerned to show the value of reason (science) and art working hand in hand to promote the well-being of all life. His writings focus on the unique creative qualities of human <u>Memory</u> which he believed hold the key to our survival as truly human beings. For reasons known only to the spiritual endowment of our race, when Primo Levi very much wanted to give up and die, his identity as a Jew and the immortal words of Dante came to his rescue, calling him to the life of a poet, a maker of words necessary for life.

End

AN UNCERTAIN HOUR

ACT ONE

(As the audience enters the theatre, they see an entirely empty stage except for a man [PRIMO LEVI] standing alone, C, facing the audience. He is modestly dressed in casual clothing typical of the Northern Italian working middle class. When the audience is settled and focused, the VOICE of an Italian fascist interrogator is heard.)

VOICE *(from offstage)*. *Partigiano!* *(Simultaneous with this shouted accusation, PRIMO mimes having his face slapped. The sound of the slap should be sharply distinct and forceful. Again from offstage, the VOICE.)* Confess, you are a partisan! *(Again PRIMO's face is slapped.)*

PRIMO. *Sono Ebreo.* I am an Italian citizen of Jewish blood.

(As soon as PRIMO utters the last words of this fatal sentence a WOMAN enters from L, singing a Sephardic Jewish lullaby to absent children, "Durme, Durme," or some other appropriate lullaby. She carries a rocking chair which she sets in place for PRIMO. The WOMAN is simply dressed. She wears a head scarf. She takes a position L and a MAN [JEAN] enters from R. He is pushing a wheelbarrow full of old shoes. He sets the wheelbarrow next to the rocking chair and takes a position R. JEAN is dressed in the garb of a prisoner of a death camp. He wears an Army prison blanket wrapped around him to protect him from a cold that is more spiritual than physical. PRIMO

goes to the wheelbarrow, selects a shoe, sits in the rocking chair, starts cleaning the old shoe with great care. As he cleans the shoe, he recites verses from Dante. The WOMAN continues to sing softly in the background.)

PRIMO. *"O Frati, O Frati...*
Considerate la vostra semenza:
fatti non foste a viver come bruti,
ma per sequir virtute e canoscenza."

(The WOMAN stops singing the lullaby. A light focuses on JEAN. JEAN lets the blanket fall and addresses the audience.)

JEAN. I don't think you properly appreciate the problem. Frankly, I don't think you even want to understand, because to understand you must trespass, push beyond the boundaries, violate the very conditions of your existence.

PRIMO. My Brothers, Consider...

JEAN. Consider this. You need to kill someone. It doesn't matter why, whether you want to, or whether you are being forced to do so by circumstances or authorities. Motives and feelings really don't matter.

PRIMO. Consider the seed that gave you life...

JEAN. I'll make a concession—you need to kill someone or else you yourself will be killed, but really this is a mere detail. In fact, I fear it will distract you from the true heart of the matter.

PRIMO. You were not made to live mindless and careless lives.

JEAN. You need to kill someone. This is your task, this is your problem. How are you going to do it?

PRIMO. You were made to know truth and to follow its path.

Act I AN UNCERTAIN HOUR Page 13

JEAN. What about using your bare hands? That's a good, honest approach. But, have you ever tried to do that, kill someone with your bare hands? It's very difficult. This method requires a great deal of physical exertion, psychological determination or powerful passion. People do not die easily. You've got to know what you're doing, and even then, it takes effort. If you find this hard to grasp conceptually, try it sometime, then you'll understand my point.

PRIMO. We have already crossed a hundred thousand dangers. With this brief time remaining to us, let us keep awake. Remember who you are. Remember the seed that gave you birth. *(The WOMAN removes the scarf covering her head. She reads a letter to PRIMO.)*

WOMAN. Dear Mr. Levi, Thank you for your reply to my letter. I never expected you to answer. I thought at best I'd get a form letter from your secretary or something like that, but I should have known better. I've tried to tell the people in my village what I saw but they won't listen to me, so, with your permission, I'm going to tell you. Then maybe someday, someday when people are ready to listen, these stories will be waiting for them.

(The WOMAN summons a BOY from offstage, leads the BOY to PRIMO. She hands the letter to the BOY who in turn hands it to PRIMO. The BOY sits on the floor in front of PRIMO. The WOMAN exits.)

PRIMO. *"O Frati, O Frati...*
  Considerate la vostra semenza:
  fatti non foste a viver come bruti,
  ma per sequir virtute e canoscenza."

BOY. The Song of Ulysses, Canto xxvi.

PRIMO. Verse?

BOY. Verse 118.

PRIMO. Bravo! *(The BOY jumps up, heads offstage.)* We're not finished.

BOY. I know. *(He's gone.)*

JEAN. Let us advance our problem to the next level of technique, as our ancestors had to, in the effort to survive, in the effort to gain a toehold for the human species in the competition of life. Let's consider using a weapon. A knife, for example. You'd think a knife would make things easier. But really not much. No, not much easier, because a knife is an extension of the hand, of our physical self, so it's still within the range of the human, so to speak, still within the range of...decency in some queer way. You still have to get close to your victim. You might smell the garlic on his breath, or the fear oozing out of his pores. This might upset your stomach or disturb the firmness of your resolution. And when you plunge the knife into his gut, blood will surely spurt out, splashing all around, perhaps even staining your favorite shirt. Yes, that's how it is when you have to deal face to face with real living human beings. Things get messy. There's no getting around that.

(As JEAN speaks the above, The BOY re-enters with a Macintosh computer setup in tow.)

PRIMO *(seeing the computer)*. That's not what I had in mind.

BOY. You promised.

PRIMO. After we finish our study of Dante's *Inferno*.

BOY. It's too long. You tricked me.

PRIMO. We're very close to the end.

Act I   AN UNCERTAIN HOUR   Page 15

- BOY. There are eight more cantos and none of them are short. Poems are supposed to be short. *(The BOY continues to set up the computer, getting it operational.)*
- JEAN. I have taught myself the ancient Japanese art of Sepuku. With a few minor adjustments, I can adapt this technical skill I've acquired for killing myself to killing someone other than myself. It is a matter of complete indifference to the technique.
- BOY. If Dante's so smart, why does he write in such funny Italian?
- PRIMO. I already explained that to you. Dante was one of the first people ever to write in Italian. You could even say he invented our language. So, of course it differs from ours. What's so surprising is how much like ours it is.
- JEAN. You don't just take a knife and shove it willy-nilly into the belly, whether your own, or a friend's, or a stranger's. It makes no difference. A belly's a belly.
- PRIMO. *"Considerate la vostra semenza:"*
- BOY. My Brothers, Consider the seed that gave you life...
- JEAN *(takes out a knife, demonstrates the technique).* First, you must learn to hold the knife tilted down at the proper angle, with the wrist perfectly relaxed, and the elbow slightly bent, like this. Second, you must position yourself in such a way that when you make your thrust deep into the gut you won't throw yourself off balance. *(Demonstrates footing for the lunge/thrust.)* Third, you must aim to hit your target in the soft part of the belly under his right rib cage just below the liver. Right here *(Demonstrates the placement of knife's cutting into the gut.)* Obviously, you don't want to hit a rib or have to make a second stab. Fourth and finally, you must thrust deep, without unbalancing your center of gravity, pull up firmly with a quick powerful twisting of the wrist, *(Demonstrates the wrist*

movement up.) then shift sharply to your left with the full strength of your arm to cut the vital veins that flow into the liver. *(Demonstrates the movement of the arm so that the knife cuts into the liver.)* Beautiful, isn't it, body, wrist, arm—a true physical poetry. You see, it's the liver that matters. If you don't cut deeply into the liver, there's a good chance the person will survive. But, if you cut sharply into the liver, he'll bleed to death very rapidly, and, all things considered, isn't that the best thing for him as well as for you. Isn't that, all things considered, the humane thing to do.

BOY. You'll be able to write lots more letters with the computer.

PRIMO. I do just fine with my pen. We're old friends. *(PRIMO takes his pen from his pocket, handles it with obvious love.)*

BOY. Nobody can read your writing.

PRIMO. *"Fatti non foste a viver come bruti"*...

BOY. You were not made to live mindless lives...

JEAN. But perhaps you are protesting to yourself that even the knife is too much trouble. You need something easier, much easier, if you have to kill someone. So, you say to yourself, let's try a gun. But, even the gun is an extension of the human body. No matter how sophisticated the gun might be. It has mass and weight. You have to carry it, you have to aim it. In short, you have to know how to use it and how to take proper care of it. You still need to be at one with it, as they say in Zen philosophy, to make it work well. It's still a tool fitted to the physics of the human body. You feel its recoil when it fires. You smell the powder. You can feel the heat it generates. The sound hurts your ears.

BOY. Why are you always cleaning those old shoes?

PRIMO. *"ma per sequir virtute e canoscenza."*

BOY. You were made to pursue knowledge and virtue.

JEAN. Now are you beginning to appreciate the problem? If you find it so difficult to kill just one person, how can you get a small number of people to kill a great many people. If our technology is merely an extension of our human physical/sensual being, it will never work. Never. Because even the most dedicated, the most hard working, the most fanatical killer will get tired. Again, if you don't believe me, try it. Take a pistol, a good, well-made Luger, and shoot a person in the back of the head, just one person every ten seconds for just one hour. Or, take a machine gun, and shoot ten people in the back every ten seconds for one hour. Do you see the problem? Do you feel the problem? It wears you down, no matter how dispassionate you are. It wears down the machines as well. And it's expensive. It's not cost effective: it uses up too much human and material resources. But worst of all, and this is the biggest problem in the whole equation, worst of all, when a person is killing thousands and thousands and thousands of persons, you begin to lose interest. *(During the following, JEAN takes the fallen Army blanket, moves toward PRIMO, places it around PRIMO's shoulders.)*

BOY. If you use the computer you can write your books much faster.

PRIMO. Faster doesn't mean better.
   *"Fatti non foste a viver come bruti,
   ma per seguir virtute e canoscenza."*

BOY. We already did that line.

PRIMO. Do it again.

BOY. Why?

PRIMO. Because it's important. "My Brothers…"

BOY. My Brothers, You were not created to live mindless lives but to follow virtue and knowledge.
He misspelled: *"conoscenza"*?

PRIMO. So you noticed. That's good. That's very good. He didn't misspell it.

BOY. Yes, he did. It's "c-*o*-n" not "c-*a*-n." I asked my teacher in school. *(The BOY spells it out.)* *"Conoscenza."* Dante's wrong.

JEAN. The boy's right, Primo. Dante is wrong.

PRIMO *(rising from the chair).* No. *(The blanket falls.)* Dante is not wrong. *(PRIMO goes over to the computer where the BOY is hacking away.)* Dante wants us to understand that knowledge and he uses this special spelling on purpose to show us the common origin of these words.

BOY. I don't know why you got this fancy MacIntosh if you don't ever want to learn how to use it?

PRIMO. I bought it so you would study Dante with me.

BOY. But I do study Dante. *(Exits to get the mail. PRIMO sits down at the computer. He begins to use it as a word processor. He writes hesitantly at first, then more confidently.)*

JEAN. Dante is wrong, Primo. For a thousand years, we've been pretending that he is right, but he is wrong.

PRIMO. When every cell of my body, when every quality of my soul longed for death, what made me quote Dante to you? What made you want to listen to me speak his words? Why did you care?

JEAN. In the blood of the young, the sap of life is a torrential urge. I wanted to believe. What were my alternatives: the blood gods of the German folk, the dead god of the Christians, the impotent god of the Jews? A philosophical poet seemed just the thing for an act of faith.

PRIMO. I wanted so much to die, and when I tried to die, his words came gushing out of my mouth. Not words of hatred or despair or self-pity. Not prayers to some unknown savior. I breathed in death and exhaled the words of a poet. My last breath became a new life for me. Dante's words saved me, Jean. And, they saved you. *(JEAN takes a shoe from the wheelbarrow. He holds it arm's length from his body.)*

JEAN. We are dead, Primo. *(Lets the shoe drop to the floor.)* Dante has merely extended the duration of our dying. He has delayed our hearing the sound of the second shoe.

PRIMO. Jean, you taught me to survive. No, you forced me to survive. You, and Lorenzo, and Steinlauf. For what reason? Out of cruelty? To prolong suffering? Why did you want to live? Why did you want me to want to live?

JEAN. We were murdered the very first moment they negated our humanity.

PRIMO. Your writings, Jean, are the most eloquent, most gentle, most humane testimonies to their utter failure to destroy the human spirit.

JEAN. Poetry is your claw, Primo, as philosophy was mine. You write to defend yourself. That I can understand. What I cannot understand is why you insist on believing that art can change us for the better. Look at the world, Primo. In the camp, you were a man without illusions. No ideology could seduce you. Neither the Marxists, nor the religious Jews, nor the Catholics. You refused to cloud your mind with theoretical excuses for the plain truth of the evil we inflict upon each other.

PRIMO. Jean, there are some things in life which are entirely of our own will and creation, but there are other things which are given to us. This has been given to me. I have tried to die. I have tried *not* to remember. But I cannot escape myself.

JEAN. Silence is the only honest response left to us. If Dante were alive today, he would not write a word. There is no vision of humanity that can redeem us from ourselves.

PRIMO. Every Wednesday I go to an elementary school to talk about writing. When I am with these young students, with these children, I can see in their eyes the thirst for knowledge, I can feel in their hearts the passion for truth, I can taste the joy of communication in their efforts to write. When I am with these children, Jean, I am like them. I remember...I remember the six-year-old boy who made a rocket ship with his first chemistry set. I remember the boy that pricked his finger so he could see his own blood, full of life, under the microscope. I remember the human being, Primo Levi, the person that wanted to discover and name every unknown star in the heavens. When I am with these children, Jean, I understand. I understand that I cannot remain silent. I must tell the stories of the people who have been entrusted to me. *(PRIMO types the name "Jean." An electronic billboard displays the name "Jean.")* Jean was fourteen when they put him in the camp. He spoke German and French which was useful, and had a good ear for picking up other languages as well, which was also useful. But Jean knew that it was even more useful not to let anyone know this. Jean was small and slight and intelligent, in short, destined for the ovens, but one of the Kapos took a liking to Jean. He could see that Jean was—exceptional. Jean knew how to "organize" things, that's a camp expression. It means knowing how to get whatever you need or whatever your Kapo wants. It means knowing how to survive. *(As JEAN speaks, PRIMO writes on the MacIntosh.)*

JEAN. I served my Kapo well. I satisfied his needs, whatever they might be—he liked his Pikolos to be young. He was a good man really, of the German criminal class who thought us all hopelessly stupid in the art of staying alive. To his credit, I must tell you he only hit us or hurt us when it was necessary to save our lives. Only once did he beat a man to death, but that too was because the man broke a rule in front of an S.S. commandant and it was either his life or the man's life. I was Jewish, but that was of no importance to me, and I don't even know if they knew that. They just picked me up on the streets one day and shipped me off, naming me a hooligan. My Kapo got me the green star of a German criminal to wear, to give me status. My job was an easy one, by comparison to the others. The only thing you had to worry about was pleasing your Kapo. If you pleased him, you lived. If not, you died. I had to make sure the barracks were kept clean, and that all the labor gangs attached to the barracks properly performed their tasks. I ladled out the soup twice a day, saving all the cabbage and other few vegetables at the bottom for the Kapo, myself, and for those I liked. I got to keep all the soup that was left over, which was whatever amount I wanted to have left over since I filled the tins. This was how I survived trading soup for whatever I or my Kapo or my friends needed. There were many Italians in my barracks, and many became my friends, but one was extraordinary. He never asked anything of me, but for some reason, he was desperate to recite to me the works of Dante. He didn't know why and I didn't know why, but he recited Dante to me until I learned almost the entire *Inferno* by heart. You can imagine how bizarre my Italian is: it's Dante-esque.

VOICE *(from offstage)*. *Selekcija! (Polish term meaning: selection.)*

(The BOY enters.)

BOY. I forgot: there's no mail today. *(The word "Selection" flashes on the electronic board. PRIMO causes the document he is working on to "crash.")* You crashed the system again.

VOICE *(from offstage)*. Selection!

BOY. You always make the same mistakes. *(PRIMO leaves the computer and walks toward the audience. He stands facing the audience.)*

ITALIAN INTERROGATOR'S VOICE *(from offstage)*. Partigiano! *(PRIMO's mimes having his face slapped. The BOY comes close to PRIMO, studies his face.)*

ITALIAN INTERROGATOR'S VOICE. Confess, you are a partisan! *(PRIMO's face is slapped again.)*

PRIMO. *Sono Ebreo.* I am an Italian citizen of Jewish blood.

VOICE *(from offstage)*. Selekcija! *(The BOY takes PRIMO by the hand, leads him back to the computer.)*

BOY. Don't worry, I'll fix it for you.

PRIMO *(directly to audience)*. My people speak a language composed of Hebrew and a form of the Piemontese dialect of Northern Italy. This unlikely marriage of tongues makes a strangely powerful, almost lyrically rugged language with deep guttural sounds and soaring vowels. To my knowledge, this language has never been written down. When I was taken to Auschwitz, the Jewish prisoners did not believe I was Jewish because I did not know their customs and could speak no Yiddish. Some thought I was a spy. They started hitting me, and screaming at me, but I couldn't understand them or speak to them. Then, this lullaby my grandmother used to sing to me came rushing out of my mouth. I didn't even know the meaning of half the words. But, when they heard the sounds of this lullaby in this strange half-Hebrew, half-Italian language, they stopped beating me. They knew I was a Jew. *(As soon as PRIMO says the word "Jew," the full ENSEMBLE form a perfect file as if in a prison camp.)*

VOICE *(from offstage). Selekcija! (According to the director's assignments, the ENSEMBLE recite the following lines. The dash indicates the line breaks for each actor.)*

— To destroy a man is difficult
  almost as difficult as to create one.

— In the middle of life's journey
  I found myself lost in a dark wood
  where I could not discover
  my way out.

— What has happened before
  has become true once more:

— The good are drowned,

— The worst survive.

— A man must be forced down low

— To know what raises him high.

— At dawn, the light of the sun fell upon us
  like Judas kissing his friend to betray him.

— The Italian guards turned their eyes away.

— Mothers prepared food for the journey.

— The Jews of Tripoli sat in a circle,
  lit ritual candles, waited for morning,
  wailing ancient lamentations.

BOY *(to the audience).* What would you do? The children must eat.

PRIMO. My people are especially fond of the Hebrew phrase, *bahalom,* in a dream. It's always tacked on to any strong affirmation—a way of making a joke against oneself when one wants something very much or believes something too much. When Ferdinand and Isabella drove the Moors out of Spain, the Inquisition gave my people the choice of converting to Catholicism or of emigrating. My people said: We shall go to Italy and make a new life, *bahalom*, a life free from anxiety and pain, *bahalom*, a life in which Jew and Gentile can live together in peace, *bahalom*. *(Pause.)* In the dialect of my people, there is no word for "sun" or "man" or "city" because there is no need for them. There are words, however, for "night," "to hide," "money," "prison." *(JEAN and the WOMAN come forward. They sing the following work camp song of the prisoners of Auschwitz.)*

THE DUET OF THE DAMNED

WOMAN. The tramp of our march is loud
    and forever
    Our faces are set and grave
    Our columns leave in perfect array
    We're always faithful and brave.

JEAN. The young tell the young only the old...

WOMAN. This is why we live
    To accept whatever fate may send
    This is how we live
    Always ready for the end.

JEAN. The old tell the old only the sick...

WOMAN. When the voice of our master roars
    We form our perfect columns.

JEAN. The strong tell the strong only the weak...

WOMAN. When the eyes of our master look our way
    We're always ready to obey.

JEAN. The skilled tell the skilled only the non-essential will be selected.

WOMAN. This is why we live

JEAN. The low numbers assure themselves that only the high numbers will be selected.

WOMAN. To accept whatever fate may send.

JEAN. The Poles say the Gypsies will be selected first.

WOMAN. This is how we live

JEAN. The Gypsies say the Russian prisoners will be selected first.

WOMAN. Always ready for the end.

JEAN. The Russian prisoners say the Jews will be selected first.

WOMAN. Work is Life
>We don't want to escape
>*Arbeit Macht Frei!*
>We want to obey or die.

JEAN. The German Jews say the non-German Jews will be selected first.

(At the BOY's prompting, sometime toward the end of the above duet, PRIMO resumes typing. He is typing the following text into the word processor, speaking the text as he types. The BOY supervises PRIMO's use of the word processor. Portions of this text should be flashed on the electronic board.)

PRIMO. Monsignor Lucchini calls me aside. He has information, solid information. This time will be different. The Holy See, the Pope Himself, has intervened. Even the Italian Fascists agree. No more Italians. His voice lowers even further. No more Italians. We are safe.

VOICE *(from offstage)*. *Selekcija!*

PRIMO. Monsignor Lucchini gives me this guarantee in the morning. In the afternoon, seven percent of the camp is selected.

JEAN *(to the audience)*. Why seven percent? Because a train is coming that evening with a new shipment of prisoners that equals seven percent of the *Haeftlings* of the camp. *(JEAN follows PRIMO through this next scene.)*

Act I   AN UNCERTAIN HOUR   Page 27

VOICE *(from offstage).* Selection!

PRIMO. Monsignor Lucchini is among the first to become smoke from the chimneys of Birkenau.

(Again the program in which PRIMO is working "crashes." A man from the ensemble, playing the role of the KAPO, forcefully grabs PRIMO from his chair, pushes him down to the floor, kicks him. The BOY sits in PRIMO's chair at the desk, works with the computer.)

BOY. You did it again. Now watch me closely. *(The BOY works at the computer during the following scene to restore the program.)*

KAPO *(to PRIMO).* Do not speak unless you are asked directly to speak. Do not let them know that you know German.

PRIMO. But, I don't know...

KAPO *(kicks PRIMO).* Do not speak unless you are asked directly to speak. *(PRIMO nods his head to indicate his understanding. KAPO lifts PRIMO up. They walk.)* If they suspect you understand German, they'll mark you for selection. *(KAPO looks at PRIMO walking.)* Keep your eyes down. Never look them in the eye. To look in the eye is a challenge, do you understand? Walk like a submissive dog with your tail between your legs. *(PRIMO obeys.)* Good. The Chief Chemical Engineer will address you in German. You must answer only those questions he directly asks you. You must answer them precisely. You must say nothing more. Do you understand? *(PRIMO nods. KAPO hits PRIMO very hard, throws him down in front of the Chief Chemical Engineer's desk.)* Haeftling 174517 [These numbers are said in German], *Herr Doktor. Er sagt er ist Chemiker.*

(The German Chief Chemical Engineer [THE BUREAU-CRAT] is reading a report containing information about PRIMO. The BUREAUCRAT is a civilian. He works for a private German company that is under contract to make synthetic rubber at Buna which is a work camp attached to Auschwitz and Birkenau.)

JEAN. If the Kapo had not hit prisoner 174517 very hard, if he had not hurt number 174517 when he presented him to the Chief Engineer, the S.S. would have noticed this and both of their lives would have been placed in jeopardy. Do you understand?

BUREAUCRAT. *Verstehen Sie?* *(PRIMO still on the floor, does not know how to answer.)*

JEAN. Please note that the Chief Engineer has addressed him in polite, formal German.

BUREAUCRAT. *Verstehen Sie?* Do you understand German?

PRIMO. I know only the German I learned from my study of chemistry books.

BUREAUCRAT. Which books?

PRIMO. Gatterman, principally.

BUREAUCRAT *(takes a book out from side of desk, sets it on desk).* Gatterman, of course. Good. Get up, please. *(PRIMO rises slowly, stands, keeps his eyes cast down.)* Where did you get your degree?

PRIMO. At Turin. 1941. *Summa Cum Laude.* *(KAPO hits PRIMO.)*

BUREAUCRAT. *Heraus!*

KAPO. *Ja wohl, Herr Doktor!* *(KAPO exits the scene. JEAN remains in the scene in an unobtrusive way.)*

BUREAUCRAT. I assure you this is as unpleasant for me as it is for you. I do not know what crimes you committed, nor do I care to know. I have a job to do here. My company has a job to do here. That is the only thing that concerns me. Do you understand?

PRIMO. *Ich verstehe.*

BUREAUCRAT. Good. Tell me, Herr Levi, how is it that a Jew could go to University and get his degree, *summa cum laude* or otherwise?

PRIMO. In Italy, Jews were not forbidden to go to University until very late, until 1943 to be exact.

BUREAUCRAT. I'm not asking you about laws.

PRIMO. One professor. From the entire faculty, one professor...was willing to teach chemistry to a Jew.

BUREAUCRAT. A brave man.

PRIMO. He said he was too old to be afraid, and that he needed a good lab assistant.

BUREAUCRAT. A practical man.

PRIMO. He took his doctorate in chemistry at Heidelberg.

BUREAUCRAT. My own *alma mater!* What's his name? Perhaps we know each other.

PRIMO. As I said, he's quite old. I'm sure you would not know each other.

BUREAUCRAT. Of course, how thoughtless of me. *(He gets up from behind his desk, moves menacingly around PRIMO.)* No matter. There's work to be done. No time for idle chatter. They give me girls, Herr Levi, stupid girls. The Poles are the worst, stupid and ugly. The French girls are all whores but at least they have some synapses firing in their silly, pretty heads. That's what I've got, Herr Levi, stupid Polish girls and French whores. They can't calibrate. They can't measure anything properly. They can't weigh anything properly. And in Berlin the paper pushers construct timetables for me while they are sipping the finest French cognac and eating the finest Bavarian sausages. *Verstehen Sie,* Herr Levi? *(He forcefully grabs PRIMO's right hand.)* Do you know what we are doing here at Buna, Herr Levi?

PRIMO. *Nein. Ich weiss nicht.*

BUREAUCRAT *(twists PRIMO's right hand so he can see a scar).* Of course not. It is of the highest secrecy. We're making synthetic rubber, Herr Levi, synthetic rubber. Or, to be precise, we are planning to make synthetic rubber, and, thus freed from our unacceptable dependence on others, we will win the war. That's what we're doing here, Herr Levi. *(Examines the scar on the fatty part of the PRIMO's palm, near the thumb.)* Good. *(The palm to PRIMO's face.)* The infallible sign. *(BUREAUCRAT shows PRIMO his own right palm.)* Only we working chemists bear these stigmata of our trade. Paper pushers don't puncture the delicate tissue of their hands with shards of broken test tubes. Los, ab!

(KAPO enters, grabs PRIMO, drags him over to where the MacIntosh computer is, throws him roughly to the floor. PRIMO rises. The BOY turns to him.)

BOY. There. Do you understand now? You must always save the file you're in before you open up another file, or else you get yourself into big trouble, and I won't always be here to help you.

PRIMO *(to the BOY).* Thank you.

BOY. When you want to merge documents, you should do it this way...*(The BOY resumes his working on the computer.)*

JEAN *(to PRIMO).* You're wasting your time.

PRIMO. I have no choice.

JEAN. They don't want to understand.

PRIMO. There are some...

Act I   AN UNCERTAIN HOUR   Page 31

JEAN. Oh, please, Primo, not you, not from someone who respects language and genuine thinking. You're not going to use that feeble word, sincere. Hitler was sincere. Sincerity is a form of sentimentality.

(As JEAN turns away from PRIMO, a light focuses on LORENZO. He is on a ladder, constructing a wall.)

LORENZO. *Cazzo!* Sonsofbitches! *(LORENZO starts to descend the ladder. PRIMO enters the scene with LORENZO.)* Up, down. Up, down. They think I'm a monkey.

PRIMO. *Tu sei Piemontese?*

LORENZO. *Was wilst du?* I don't like nobody looking at me.

PRIMO. You are Piemontese. Your dialect. Your accent.

LORENZO. Maybe yes, maybe no, but you, you definitely Piemontes', and you're late. Get the cement ready. You know how to do this work? Of course not, why would they give me somebody who knows how to do this? You put the cement in the bucket. You do like this...*(Mimes swinging the bucket between his legs to gain the momentum to lift it up onto his shoulders. He hands the bucket to PRIMO. PRIMO tries, but the weight of the bucket is so great it throws PRIMO off balance.)* Porca La Madonna! Never mind. You too weak to do this. *(Air raid sirens start to wail. LORENZO grabs his hat and tool kit. To PRIMO.)* Subito! *(Directs PRIMO to a large sewer drainage pipe that sits abandoned in a pile of construction materials. They enter it, using it as their air raid shelter.)* The Americans by day. The British by night. Where is the great Luftwaffe? Ah, yes, excuse me, Signore Goering, I always forget, your planes are too busy winning the war someplace else. *(Hands PRIMO his lunch bag.) Mangia. (PRIMO is reluctant to take it, but LORENZO's second prodding and his hunger overcome his hesitancy. He eagerly opens the bag. He finds cheeses and olives and salami from Italy.)* Where are you from? *(Sounds of bombs dropping.)*

PRIMO. Torino? You?

LORENZO. Fossano.

PRIMO. Fossano. I have family there.

LORENZO. Everybody in Italy has family everywhere. That's the first thing you learn when you leave Fossano. And the second thing you learn is that every Italian everywhere knows somebody who knows somebody who knows your family. You know how to read, write?

PRIMO. Yes, of course. *(LORENZO hands PRIMO a letter.)* I'm sorry. I meant no offense.

LORENZO. Read.

PRIMO. My dearest son, Lorenzo, I'm fine so don't worry. Everyone is fine so don't worry. Your cousin, Sergio, had another gall bladder attack. They say next time they going to take it out. I tell him, no hospital, no cutting. He should eat better. Stay well, my son, stay well. Waiting for you to come home, your loving mother.

LORENZO. My mother, she just like me. We don't like words too much. Sometimes we say maybe two, three words to each other all day. *(Pause.)* You write for me, for my mother in Fossano. I tell you, you write. OK?

PRIMO. I'm honored but...

LORENZO. Don't worry. I give you paper. I get you nice pen, too. Don't worry. No one know you do this. And you read to me my mother's letters. I don't like everyone in the barracks knowing my business. OK?

PRIMO. OK. *(He stops eating, gathers the food, tries to hand the remaining food back to LORENZO.)* Thank you. It's very good.

LORENZO. Eat. The Americans no going give you much more time.

PRIMO. It's your lunch, and it's obviously very special food from home.

LORENZO. Shut up, eat. *(PRIMO resumes eating. LORENZO looks out of the pipe to see his wall.)*

PRIMO. Your wall, it's OK?

LORENZO. Sure. Sure she's OK. They have to hit her right on the nose with one of their bombs to upset her very much. You like my little home? Cozy, no?

PRIMO. It would be better if it were underground. More protection.

LORENZO. No. Not better. I like to hear the bombs. Boom. Boom. Lovely music. And I like to see my way out. I don't like to be crowded into a hole. I need air to breathe. When I want, I look out, see the sky. No one bother me, everybody underground, but me. *Capisch'?*

PRIMO. *Si, capisco.* But, you're not afraid?

LORENZO. Of many things, yes. Of these bombs, no. They no bother me. You? You afraid?

PRIMO. Of many things, yes. Of these bombs, yes. I must tell you, you've misunderstood something, I wasn't sent here to work for you. You can be executed for talking to me.

LORENZO. If the Gestapo want to kill me, they don't need a reason. *(Hands PRIMO an Italian Army Alpine mess tin with water in it.)* Drink. *Acqua pura*, not that stinking mud they pipe in from the river.

PRIMO *(drinks some of the water)*. It's distilled.

LORENZO. *Si, distillata.* From the tanks in the factory. So far that's all they make there. Water. They supposed to make rubber. That's a big military secret. The Gestapo can kill me two times for knowing this. But, so far, no rubber. You ask me. Never. Never going to be rubber from this factory. I know they kill Jews in the ovens in Birkenau. They can kill me four times for knowing this. These German sonofabitches have lots a good reasons to kill me.

PRIMO. Why do you make good walls for these...German sonsofbitches?

LORENZO. I make good walls, only good walls, that's all I make.

PRIMO. So they won't kill you, so they'll let you get packages from home.

LORENZO. My father, he was a stonemason. My grandfather, he was a stonemason. They only make good walls. I work for Swiss sonsofabitches and French sonsofabitches and now I work for German sonsofabitches. I only make good walls.

PRIMO. It's not the same.

LORENZO. You got a girlfriend, a sweetheart?

PRIMO. No.

LORENZO. That's no good. You should have a girlfriend.

PRIMO. It makes no difference.

LORENZO. A young man like you, you should have a girlfriend. *(Beat.)* You're right. These sonsofbitches are real sonsofbitches. When I was in France, the Gestapo, they put a gun to my head—you stupid Italian sonofabitch you come with us. That's how I get here. *(Beat.)* You have known women?

PRIMO. No.

LORENZO. No?

PRIMO. No.

LORENZO. What a world! *(PRIMO hands the Italian Army mess tin to LORENZO.)* No, no. That's for you. Tomorrow, you come here. You leave it here. I fill it up for you, with *zuppa*. Good soup. We make our own, in the barracks. You know how we Italians are. We have no stomach for somebody else's cooking. *(Pause.)* Make me a promise...come *ti chiam'?*

PRIMO. Primo.

LORENZO. Make me a promise, Signore Primo, make me this promise, promise me you leave this place, you go back to Italy, you know a woman.

PRIMO. How can I make such a promise?

LORENZO. And, with God's help, you have some children. Promise me this.

PRIMO. How can I? *(The all-clear sirens start to wail.)*

LORENZO. You ask me why I build good walls for German sonsofbitches. I only know one thing: how to make a good wall. That's all I know. If anyone tries to tell me anything about this, I take my hat and tools and leave. Walls, good walls, this is the only thing I know. But you, you are educated. You know many things; you can do many things. The strength of life is very great in your eyes. You must leave this place. You must go back to Italy. You must know a woman. Otherwise, the sonsofbitches win. Do you understand? Otherwise, the sonsofbitches win. Promise.

PRIMO. I promise.

LORENZO. *Bene.* Remember. Tomorrow you put the mess tin here. I fill it up for you. *(They exit the pipe.)*

VOICE *(from offstage).* Halt!

LORENZO. Him? He's helping me with the wall, but he's too weak. I need somebody else, somebody with muscle. Otherwise, up down, up down. *Versteh, (Loudly.)* you sonofabitch. *(Soto voce.)*

BOY. What was Lorenzo's last name?

PRIMO. He doesn't have one.

BOY. Everybody has a last name. You just don't want to tell me. *(Exits to get the mail.)*

PRIMO. One day toward the end of the war with the Russians pressing hard on the Auschwitz-Buna-Birkenau camps, some German sonofabitch with charts and blueprints in his hands tried to tell Lorenzo something about a wall. That night, Lorenzo put on his cap, grabbed his tool kit, and walked out of the camp. Without passports, papers, permits, or anything to identify him, he walked all the way back to Italy. First he went to Turin, found out where my mother was hiding with some peasants in the mountains, went to her, told her not to worry, told her her son would soon be home. Then he went to Fossano. He walked in, kissed his mother, went into the only bedroom in the house, closed the door, went to sleep. When he woke up he ate a great deal, still he said nothing, and went back to sleep. After a few days, he got a job building walls at a construction site outside of Fossano. It took him two hours to walk there and two hours to walk back. One day an Italian sonofabitch tried to say something to him about a wall. Lorenzo put on his cap, picked up his bag of tools, and left, without speaking a word. A week later they found him lying under a tree in the countryside. He was wide awake. He said nothing. They took him to the hospital. The doctors said there was nothing wrong with Lorenzo that they could see, except of course that he was dying. When he died a few weeks later, on the line of the form where the hospital requires you to list a cause of death...well, they simply left it blank.

(PRIMO takes the pen LORENZO gave him, fondles it lovingly. The BOY enters, hands PRIMO the mail.)

PRIMO. Thank you.

Act I	AN UNCERTAIN HOUR	Page 37

BOY. You get a lot of mail. My mother says people shouldn't bother you so much.

PRIMO. We all need some one to listen to us, some one to care about what we think and feel.

BOY. My mother says they shouldn't bother you. *(Moves back toward the computer, passes by the wheelbarrow full of old shoes. He picks one up, turns toward PRIMO.)* Why do you keep these old shoes? They're all worn out. *(The BOY carelessly places the shoe back in the wheelbarrow causing it to fall to the floor.)*

PRIMO *(sharply in anger). St' Attento!* Everything in life deserves our care and respect. Have you learned nothing from your study of Dante?

BOY. But it's just an old shoe.

PRIMO. In everything you do, everything, you must always be careful. *(PRIMO picks up the shoe, embraces it with affection.)*

BOY. It's all worn out.

PRIMO. Yes, this shoe is old and worn, but it still has life in it. It has shared its life with me, adapting itself to my foot, to the way I bear weight, to the way I walk. This shoe, all of these shoes are part of me, part of my life. I must take care of them, choose the right soap, the right conditioners, the right polish. I must help them to live just as they have helped me to live.

BOY. I still think you should get some new shoes. I'm going to make something for you so you can write all those people and not have to work so hard. Don't worry, it'll be easy to use. You'll like it. *(The BOY resumes working at the computer.)*

PRIMO *(to the audience).* How naive we were, like boy scouts, running off into the mountains to join up with the partisans. We didn't even know where they were. I hadn't ever held a gun in my hands. I thought that by saying I was a Jew they wouldn't shoot me for being a partisan. *(Laughs.)* I played a good joke on myself, don't you think?

(PRIMO goes to the rocking chair, sits. A man from the ensemble playing the role of the GERMAN-JEWISH PRISONER moves to extreme R where in semi-darkness he takes off his clothes. He places the clothes carefully between his legs so that they do not touch the muddy ground and so that they will not be stolen. His back is to the audience. He mimes washing himself. He washes himself carefully. There is no soap. It is very cold. The water is very cold, dirty, and foul smelling. When he is finished washing, he washes his clothes. He puts them back on while still wet.)

PRIMO. Uncle Thanks-be-to-God had a large parrot, a gift from his father-in-law who was a sea captain. The parrot came from Guyana, and was very colorful. Someone had taught it to say, *nosce te ipsum,* which is Latin for "Know Thyself."

BOY *(turns toward PRIMO)*. Why didn't you run away?

PRIMO. In Greek it's *gnoti seauton.* Know thyself: that's what the Oracle said in response to the philosopher's question.

BOY. Why didn't you run away?

GERMAN-JEW *(turning toward PRIMO)*. Wash! *(PRIMO, rises from the rocking chair, shoe in hand. He enters the scene of the GERMAN-JEW washing.)*

PRIMO. Why should I? It's senseless.

GERMAN-JEW. You must. You must obey the regulations. Wash. Walk erect. March in step.

Act I   AN UNCERTAIN HOUR   Page 39

PRIMO. You Germans are all alike, Jew or Gentile. You cherish your systems and your discipline even in the face of absolute absurdity.

GERMAN-JEW *(grabs PRIMO and forcibly washes him. As he does so, PRIMO drops the shoe he is carrying).* We must wash our faces with foul-smelling water. We must dry ourselves with wet clothes. Not for the sake of Prussian discipline, not to please our Nazi masters...

PRIMO. Why? *(The BOY, having noticed PRIMO drop the shoe, gets up from the computer, picks up the shoe.)*

BOY. Why didn't you run away?

GERMAN-JEW. To stay alive.

BOY. Why didn't you run away? Why?

PRIMO *(to GERMAN-JEW).* Why?

GERMAN-JEW. Not to begin to die.

PRIMO and BOY. Why? *(GERMAN-JEW releases PRIMO. PRIMO finishes washing himself on his own. As he dries himself, he returns to the BOY.)* I didn't want to wash. I had to learn to want to and how to do it. The water was dirty and freezing cold. The floor was all mud. We had to hold our clothes between our knees. The cold wind came through the gaps between the planks of the bare walls. I hated the cold. I hated the Germans for making me cold, and I didn't want to do anything they said, even if, even if they were right. I wanted to use these precious minutes before they marched us off to work or death for something meaningful to me, like looking at the sky.

BOY. Once I drew a picture of the sky. I made all the clouds pink and purple. But my teacher said clouds were supposed to be white. I told her I'd seen purple and pink clouds many times. *(The BOY hands the shoe to PRIMO.)*

GERMAN-JEW. And your shoes, Primo, your shoes must be kept clean. You must clean them everyday, twice a day, three times a day, as often as there is need. Your shoes are your life. If your shoes become damaged, your feet get injured, and you won't last a day, not a day. We must live, Primo. That is our single duty. We must live. *(PRIMO regards the shoe with affection.)*

PRIMO *(to the BOY and to audience)*. This German Jew, who came to the camp in his own private rail car with plush, dark red, upholstered seats. This German Jew who walked so proudly through the gate with his uniform perfectly clean and pressed, his iron cross, given to him by the Kaiser himself, shining so brilliantly in the sun. Some soldiers saluted as he passed. Even the S.S. stepped aside. He walked proudly through the gate while his entire family was driven like sheep into the line destined for the chimney. This man, Friedrich Steinlauf, risked his life to make me wash.

JEAN. A Jew who is more German than a German: Poof, a puff of smoke belching from a chimney. A Jew who is more religious than God himself: Poof, a puff of smoke belching from a chimney. A Jew who believes nothing but works for justice for all: Poof, a puff of smoke belching from a chimney. And the same is true today for Jew and non-Jew alike. Evil does not discriminate.

(A MAN and a WOMAN from the ensemble set up a portable blackboard on which there is a drawing of an enormous louse. They mime cleaning themselves of lice.)

PRIMO. If you mix ashes with sand, you can rub the dirt and the lice off your body.

BOY. Ashes are dirty.

PRIMO. Actually, they make a very good cleanser. Of course, it was impossible to get rid of the lice entirely because they lay their eggs under your skin and we had no soap or chemicals to kill their eggs. But, no matter how tired or sick we were, we had to look for lice everyday. If you hold your clothes very close to a fire, you can kill the adult lice. They swell up and burst from the heat. They make this popping sound like kernels of corn popping in the skillet. In the latrine the Germans had placed this enormous drawing of a louse. Under the picture was written: *Eine Laus, dein Tod:* a louse, your death. It's important to kill the lice because they can make you very sick.

JEAN. *So bist du rein, so gehst du ein.*

PRIMO. You see, the Germans didn't want us to die until they wanted us to die.

BOY. Draw me a picture of the camp. And I'll show you how you could've escaped. *(PRIMO draws the plan of the camp, showing the barbed wire, the guard towers, the wooden houses.)*

JEAN. The S.S. consulted the best nutritionists in Germany to determine the most efficient means of feeding the slaves of their empire. At first, they rationed 600 calories for each *Haeftling*, to be given in the form of a soup two times a day. At this rate, an average human being, so they calculated, given the harsh weather, harsh work, and harsh treatment, would die in six weeks, which time-frame suited their schedule for both labor and extermination. Then, when labor started to become scarcer, they doubled the calories to 1200 a day to increase the life span to six months. This was the ration when Primo arrived at Auschwitz, 1200 calories. But, the Gestapo hadn't counted on Lorenzo, who for six months, until he escaped, gave Primo an additional portion of soup. Still not enough to enable an "average man" to survive much longer than the planned six months, but Primo wasn't an "average" man. Just one of the many small errors in the calculations of the technicians.

(The WOMAN enters. She is singing the Sephardic Ladino lullaby, "Durme, Durme." After the first verse is sung, the BOY enacts the following. The WOMAN continues to sing softly in the background.)

BOY *(goes to the blackboard, draws on it in pictures what he says in words).* When it got dark, I would sneak out, kill one of the guards, take his rifle, shoot out the light in the tower, crawl under the wire, and run real fast into the forest. *(As the WOMAN sings, JEAN hands PRIMO a very heavy wooden pail to carry. The pail is full of soup for the prisoners of the camp. PRIMO finds the weight of the pail overwhelming.)*

PRIMO. I cannot do it.

JEAN. Walk straight.

PRIMO. I'm exhausted. I can't move another step.

JEAN. The Kapo will beat you to death.

PRIMO. I don't care. I just want to rest. *(With his right arm JEAN helps PRIMO lift the large wooden pail by its handle. With his left arm he braces himself against PRIMO. PRIMO does the mirror image of this tactic for carrying the heavy load. Thus they walk, carrying the pail, each braced against the other.)*

JEAN. Primo, keep your shoulders high. Shift the weight to me. Keep your eyes straight ahead. *(The WOMAN stops singing. She now participates directly in the scene.)*

WOMAN. Brothers,

PRIMO. *"O Frati, O Frati...*

WOMAN. We have already crossed a hundred thousand dangers.

PRIMO. *"O Frati, dissi…*Jean turns toward me. I must remember. I must remember each word exactly, exactly as it is written.

WOMAN. *"Considerate…*

PRIMO. *"Considerate la vostra semenza…*Jean's eyes. So young. So new to the camp. Sadness has not yet cut deep to the abyss behind the dilating pupils.

WOMAN. Brothers, We have already crossed a hundred thousand dangers. With this brief time remaining to us, let us keep awake. Remember who you are, Remember the seed that gave you birth.

JEAN. *Zuppa, Campo, Acqua.*

PRIMO. That's all the Italian he knows.

WOMAN. *"Considerate la vostra semenza:*
    Fatti non foste a viver come bruti,
    ma per seguir virtute e canoscenza.

PRIMO. How can I make him understand. How can I make him understand when I don't understand myself, when I only know that I must speak these words to him and make him understand them? What possible meaning could this medieval poem, a Christian poem, have for him? Or for me?

JEAN. "My Brothers, Oh My Brothers, Consider the source of your being: you have not been made to live brutish lives, but to pursue virtue and true knowledge." I know more Italian than you think. *(JEAN frees himself and PRIMO from the heavy burden, placing the pole and the pail on the ground.)*

PRIMO. I wonder: in all the history of the world has poetry ever saved a life before?

JEAN. Two lives. If you had fallen, my life would also be forfeit. But, it is not by poetry alone that a man lives. *(JEAN dips a soup ladle deep into the pail to collect what little vegetables lie at the bottom of the watery brew. Hands the ladle to PRIMO.)* Eat. *(PRIMO carefully puts the ladle to his lips. The WOMAN resumes singing the lullaby.)*

VOICE *(from offstage)*. Selekcija! *(PRIMO mimes having his face slapped. He drops the ladle.)*

BOY. Why didn't you escape?

VOICE *(from offstage)*. Selection! *(Again PRIMO's face is slapped.)*

PRIMO. *Warum?*

BOY. Why?

JEAN *(directly to the audience)*. Hier gibt es kein Warum.

WOMAN *(stops singing)*. Here there is no Why.

END OF ACT ONE

ACT TWO

AT RISE: *The WOMAN is singing "Oifn Pripetshik," a Yiddish lullaby. PRIMO LEVI is sitting in the rocking chair. He is cleaning a shoe. PRIMO addresses the audience.*

PRIMO. This is my grandmother's chair. My mother gave birth to me on this very spot, on this very spot on which this old chair sits. They told me the most wonderful stories as they cradled me in their arms.

(JEAN summons the TECHNICIANS.)

THE DUET OF THE TECHNICIANS

TECHNICIAN 1. I'm not trying to gain your sympathy. Things have gone far beyond that. I don't even know why I'm telling you this. I guess every human being wants to be understood. I'm not at all a complicated person. I was flattered. Surely, you can understand that. I felt honored. Yes, honored, that such important people would call upon me to solve a problem for them. You must understand that much, how it feels to be a little person in a little position with very little promise of promotion or recognition. Yes, praise is more important to me than money. I.G. Farben is a very large company and I, I was merely one of thousands. My special interest, since I was a kid, happened to be pyrotechnics. I don't know why. I just enjoyed it. I was always making up powders to blow up glass bottles, testing chemicals to see which ones would generate combustion, fast or slow or for how long or how hot. I understand fire. One day, these government people came to me right in the plant, right in front of everybody, and they made a great show of respect for me. It felt like for once in my whole life I was appreciated for what I knew and liked and knew how to do. And the problem was interesting, a challenge, not like my regular work for Farben. They needed a way of burning human bodies so that nothing remained but the finest of ashes, so that not a trace, not the slightest trace of evidence could ever be discovered, even by the most sophisticated techniques, to prove that these bodies ever existed. I, I didn't want to know anything about these bodies. It wasn't my place. I just wanted to show my art. They said, Can you do this? I said, Sure. Sure I can. It is possible. My heart beat so wildly I couldn't sleep for days. I was feverish. But never, never had I been more happy in all my life. There was a good chance, a better than good chance really, that I would fail. But that secret fear I kept silent in my heart. Sure, I said, sure I can do this.

TECHNICIAN 2. The S.S. and the Army, because they are soldiers, and think like soldiers, thought they could simply shoot everybody. Well, this is stupid and time consuming, and a great waste of ammunition and fighting men. We didn't need soldiers to kill people. We needed a method—a simple, efficient, clean method, easily employed, and cheap. So, when they came to me with this problem, I told them exactly what I thought: this is no business for soldiers; this is work for professionals trained in the practical specializations of the applied sciences. They were impressed by my direct and clear manner and my outstanding record, of course, so they immediately assigned me to my new position and my superiors at Farben promoted me and raised my pay.

TECHNICIAN 1. The soldiers were machine gunning the naked bodies in front of open ditches which the people to be killed dug beforehand. The force of the bullets pushed the bodies forward into the ditch. Then the soldiers poured petrol over the bodies and set them ablaze. This seems efficient and effective, but it is not, as anyone who has burned things knows. The top burns, but the bottom and the middle do not burn, so you have to keep turning over the bodies to get them to combust properly by exposing them to the air. This is a great waste of time and of precious petrol which was already in short supply.

TECHNICIAN 2. I must admit my first idea was not a very good one, although it seemed very good in the mind, elegant even, because it made use of what had to be done anyway, killing two birds with one stone as the saying goes. The Army used trucks to convey the people to the camps. So, how simple, I thought. I had the soldiers run the truck's exhaust pipes into the cargo sections of the trucks which I had hermetically sealed, so that by the time the trucks got to the camps, the people would be all dead from carbon monoxide asphyxiation, Sounds good, doesn't it?

TECHNICIAN 1. Fire requires oxygen. Everyone knows this, but they don't think properly about how to get the oxygen to the right places at the right times. I conducted a series of experiments. The first experiments were done on patients from a nearby mental hospital. They were asphyxiated in the back of Army cargo vans as they were being driven to my experimental camp. Most of them were dead by the time they arrived. Those that were still alive were shot in the back of the head. Now, this was my first innovative idea: we must stack the bodies in such a way that the air can whip through them, thus burning them quickly and totally. So, I had the soldiers build large wooden tiered platforms and had the bodies placed in a pyramid-like form with layers of scrap wood and other non-essential materials separating the layers in such a way as to allow fresh air to mix freely throughout the pyramid.

TECHNICIAN 2. But, my idea didn't work well enough. First, it was too difficult to seal the cargo holds. Second, the truck engines didn't generate sufficient quantities of carbon monoxide. Third, the trips to the camps were often not long enough to give the carbon monoxide time to work. I tried sealing the vans better and added more gas engines to the trucks, just for the purpose of making more carbon monoxide. But this method didn't work well either. The next step was obvious. Farben, my employers, manufactured a very powerful insecticide, Zyclon B, on which I had been previously working before my promotion to my new position. My experiments with Zyclon B demonstrated that this insectcide could kill people very quickly if it were properly volatilized, which was easy enough to do, and if, of course, people were forced to breathe it. Science is like this, you know, in the course of finding out one thing you find out so many other things. It's serendipitous, really.

TECHNICIAN 1. But, my idea didn't work well enough. Oh, it worked much better than burning bodies in ditches, and it saved great quantities of petrol, but, you see, as the fire built in intensity, the tiers collapsed, thus preventing the air from circulating and thus some parts of human bodies remained detectable, which defeated the whole purpose of the enterprise.

TECHNICIAN 2. My idea was very simple, and simple ideas are always the best ones. I used the same Army trucks. But this time I had the soldiers drop specially designed pellets

Act II AN UNCERTAIN HOUR Page 49

of Zyclon B through hatches cut into the roofs of the cargo holds. Upon impact, the pellets broke open mixing insecticide with other chemicals, thus creating a most efficacious poisonous gas. With this method, all the people in the cargo holds died, and in record time, I might add, a mere matter of seconds. Needless to say, I.G. Farben was delighted to be selling huge quantities of its insecticide to the German Army. My Christmas bonus that year was five times the previous year's.

TECHNICIAN 1. Our experiments had used up all the mentally and emotionally defective people in the German hospitals, so now we had to use bodies of sick people, both old and young. I didn't like this idea at first. I thought we should wait for prisoners or criminals. But, this procedure proved to be the breakthrough in concept that I had been struggling for. Quite by accident, as I was burning various stacks of bodies, trying to use the minimum amount of materials and trying to avoid the collapsing phenomenon, I discovered something quite amazing: if you stack thin bodies on top of fat bodies, that is, if you stack bodies composed mostly of muscle and bones on top of bodies composed mostly of fat, if you stacked them up one on top of the other, supporting them with posts so you can go as high as you can without affecting air flow, and if you coat each layer of bodies with just the right quantity of easily combustible and inexpensive materials, then all the human bodies will burn steadily and thoroughly, leaving a most pure and rarified ash. If they hadn't given me the bodies of sick Germans to work with, of young and old, fat and thin, I would never have figured out this method.

TECHNICIAN 2. Once this principle was established, it was a simple step to prepare larger cannisters of Zyclon B for larger chambers capable of accommodating several hundred people at a time.

TECHNICIAN 1. You see, fat burns more slowly and more consistently than does muscle or bone, so it provides a steady temperature, while muscle and bone reach a flash point, in a manner of speaking, and burn off more quickly, but far less predictably, and cannot be relied upon to keep a fire going at the proper temperature over the proper length of time. So, as you can see, you can use these two facts to complement each other and make a most efficient fire. I must admit to you, the night after I demonstrated this method to my satisfaction, that was the very first night in over three months that I slept the whole night through.

TECHNICIAN 2. Once these principles were established, the details could be left to engineers. We practical scientists had done our work: we had demonstrated the proper methods.

TECHNICIANS 1 and 2 *(antiphonally)*.
— Because of the systematic soundness of our methods,
— Because of the meticulous care with which each detail was considered and arranged,
— Ten thousand human bodies could be gassed and burned to a pure, clean ash,
— A life-nourishing ash to enrich the soil of the Polish countryside,
— Nothing wasted,
— Everything used,
— The hair,
— The teeth,
— The skin,
— Every day,
— Seven days a week, 365 days a year, ten thousand bodies could be so handled.
— Amazing!

(PRIMO rises from the rocking chair, enters the office of a BUREAUCRAT, the Chief Chemical Engineer for I.G. Farben.)

BUREAUCRAT. Ah, Herr Levi, so good to meet you. I've read your book.

PRIMO. You are one of the few who has.

BUREAUCRAT. Well, that's understandable, isn't it? We've got a lot of work to do. Too much dwelling on the past could sap our strength, undermine our resolve. It is necessary now to build a new future.

PRIMO. We cannot build a truly new future if we forget what must be remembered.

BUREAUCRAT. Herr Levi, we human animals need to have positive beliefs. It is not healthy for us to dwell on the negative.

PRIMO. The truth is neither positive nor negative. It is simply necessary.

BUREAUCRAT. Psychological studies clearly demonstrate that people function better when they have something positive they can believe in.

PRIMO. Even when those beliefs require us to close our ears, shut our eyes, harden our hearts.

BUREAUCRAT. Herr Levi, you have chosen a poetic way of expressing this fact. I would not choose to say it that way. I would say we cannot eliminate illusion or delusion from our essential nature. The only thing that matters is how to promulgate the appropriate faith, how to make credible the dreams that best elicit the energies of the people to make the kind of society we wish to live in. Ultimately, that is best for everyone.

PRIMO. No, not for everyone. Such a society has no room for me, or for people like me.

BUREAUCRAT. When you made the move from science to art...

PRIMO. I never abandoned science.

BUREAUCRAT. We are not always the best judges of our own work. When we are too emotionally involved, we lose perspective.

PRIMO. My art is another way of discovering and communicating the truth.

BUREAUCRAT. You express what you feel compelled to speak. Others see things differently; they see the whole picture, not just a personal view.

PRIMO. The truth must be embraced wherever it is found, no matter how disturbing that might be. The artist is very much like the scientist. Ultimately, his personal truth, as you call it, will be judged in the light of universal history. Your opinion makes a mockery of science, which you claim to serve. It destroys the very basis for truth. It renders meaningless every person's effort to know, to speak, to be understood.

BUREAUCRAT *(pause)*. I know your book is not fiction. I know you write of what happened to you, but re-building a nation is very much like a war-time situation—the focus of the people mustn't be scattered, their energies mustn't be dissipated.

PRIMO. You were at Buna.

BUREAUCRAT *(pause)*. Yes, but, I never knew these things.

PRIMO. You knew.

BUREAUCRAT. No, I did not know.

PRIMO. The smell of burning flesh is unmistakable, especially to a chemist.

BUREAUCRAT. Yes, of course, you're correct, I knew that fact...I knew the facts but not the interpretation. Certainly you can appreciate that. As a man of science you know the difference between fact and meaning. I was told the bodies were the victims of typhus and scarlet fever and...

PRIMO. You knew.

BUREAUCRAT. Herr Levi, your company specializes in an enamel for coating copper wires. Our own chemists here at Farben have thus far been unable to match the quality of your product. In fact, we are having great trouble analyzing its composition. I understand you worked at your company on the making of these enamels before...

PRIMO. ...my deportation to Auschwitz. Yes, I did.

BUREAUCRAT. I myself tried to analyze it—quite an unusual formula, all sorts of odd ingredients, seemingly irrelevant to enamel. Very strange, very strange indeed, and when we put these chemicals together they make something very unlike enamel, let alone a good enamel. As one chemist to another...

PRIMO. You're not asking me to give away my company's trade secrets, are you?

BUREAUCRAT. Herr Levi, it is absolutely certain, merely a matter of a few months, that we at Farben will develop our own enamel, equal to or better than yours, but the fact is, the fact is that right now yours is the best available. So until our German scientists have overcome this problem, *(Hands PRIMO a sheet of paper.)* these are our needs: quantities, dates of delivery, price limits. Can your company meet these specifications and timetables?

PRIMO. *Aber naturlich, Herr Doktor.* But, just in case your German scientists are unable to produce a better enamel, our Italian chemists will keep ample quantities readily available for you.

(PRIMO mimes going up to a huge vat of chemicals being cooked into enamel. An ITALIAN CHEMICAL ENGINEER

greets PRIMO. The ENGINEER hands PRIMO a sheet of paper.)

PRIMO. *Grazie,* Signore Ingegnere, I know this formula quite well. *(PRIMO hands the sheet of paper back to the ENGINEER. PRIMO eyes the enamel, sniffs it, listens to it.)*

ENGINEER. Signore Levi, is something wrong?

PRIMO. Listen. *(The ENGINEER puts his ear close to the vat as does PRIMO.)* Do you hear it?

ENGINEER. Si, Signore Levi, but that is how it is supposed to sound. *(The ENGINEER makes a sucking, popping sound.)*

PRIMO. Some copper wire, please. *(The ENGINEER hands PRIMO some wire. PRIMO dips the wire into the vat. He examines how the enamel covers the wire and falls off the wire.)*

ENGINEER. Signore Levi, I assure you...

PRIMO. Look. Look how it sticks.

ENGINEER. Signore Levi, our enamel is the best in the world, the very best. No air bubbles, no pitting.

PRIMO. You see how the enamel drips? It collects at the tip, increases in weight, then, when gravity gains the upper hand, plop!

ENGINEER. Plop?

PRIMO. Si, plop!

ENGINEER. Signore Levi, I assure you...

PRIMO. Just like my mother's best sauce cooking on the stove. Very rich. Not watery. Sticks to the pasta.

ENGINEER. I told my wife the very thing. A good chemist is like a good cook. To make a good enamel, you need the eye, the ear, the nose, and the hand of a good chef.

Act II   AN UNCERTAIN HOUR   Page 55

PRIMO. Yes, exactly. And this batch, Signore lngegnere, this batch of enamel which you are cooking is perfetto, perfetto.

ENGINEER. *Grazie*, Signore. *(PRIMO smiles, returns to his rocking chair, resumes cleaning shoes, speaks to the BOY.)*

PRIMO. You see, the scientists at Farben were able to analyse our enamel. They were able to break it down into all of its component elements, but what they were not able to do was to understand the actual chemistry of the ingredients, how the elements actually interact when they're cooked together.

BOY. They still haven't figured it out?

PRIMO. They still come to us to buy their enamel. *(PRIMO laughs.)* And everytime they come, they always say: This is our last order, our scientists will soon develop an enamel better than yours.

BOY. They must be stupid.

PRIMO. On the contrary, they are very smart, too smart. That is their weakness. They are not humble enough to put their noses into the chemical soup. They don't use their eyes and ears. They think too much. Your mother is smarter than they are.

BOY. My mother doesn't even know how to spell.

PRIMO. When your mother goes to the market to buy tomatoes to make marinara sauce, what does she do?

BOY. I hate going shopping with her.

PRIMO. That wasn't my question.

BOY. She takes too much time.

PRIMO. What is she doing with her time?

BOY. I don't know.

PRIMO. Yes, you do.

BOY. First she looks at them, then she shakes her head, like this, *(Shakes his head to indicate disapproval.)* then Mr.

Donatelli gets all upset and says, What's wrong, Signora, the tomatoes are beautiful.

PRIMO. Go on. What does she do then?

BOY. Then she smells them, each one, she puts her nose right on them. *(Pause.)* You know what I think?

PRIMO. What? What do you think she's doing?

BOY. I think she's trying to get Mr. Donatelli to lower the price. That's what she's doing, I'm sure of it.

PRIMO *(laughs)*. Yes, Yes. That's true. But she is doing something else, something the chemists at Farben don't understand.

BOY. Well, sometimes, she even sticks her finger into the tomatoes. This gets Mr. Donatelli very upset.

PRIMO. Why does your mother do this?

BOY. I told you why: She wants him to lower the price.

PRIMO. No, your mother has another reason—a very good reason. You say you want to be a writer like me, then put yourself in her shoes.

BOY *(takes his time)*. She must be trying to figure out if the tomatoes will make a good sauce.

PRIMO. Bravo! And you see how she did it! Unlike the German scientists, your mother knows that, in actuality, no two tomatoes are exactly the same. Your mother knows that there is only one way to tell whether the tomatoes are right for the job. You must look at them, smell them, and, yes, even taste them. That is what the chemists at Farben do not know how to do. They rely on a recipe; they don't taste the sauce.

BOY. I don't think anyone would enjoy tasting enamel.

PRIMO. Have your little joke on me, but I know you understand my meaning.

BOY. Our sense of taste comes mostly from our sense of smell. You already taught me that.

Act II   AN UNCERTAIN HOUR   Page 57

PRIMO. So, then, use your imagination. Why have the chemists at I.G. Farben failed to make a better enamel?

BOY. Because they've forgotten something.

PRIMO. Yes, they have forgotten something. And what have they forgotten?

BOY. They've forgotten that a good chemist is like a good cook. Maybe they should go shopping with my mother.

PRIMO. Good idea! They should watch her shop and watch her cook. They've forgotten that science is done by a human person, that the practice of science is an art, an art that requires the active involvement of your whole being: your body, your mind, your soul, your imagination, your heart. Science without a heart...*(He pauses.)* Science without a heart...How will I ever get anyone to understand?

BOY. I almost forgot: it's time to get the mail. *(Exits.)*

PRIMO *(to the audience).* In the year 1943 just before I fled to the mountains to join the partisans, my company asked me to solve a problem they were having with the making of their enamels. I quickly figured out that the problem was that the chemicals we were using were defective. But, what could you do? Italy was at war. Defective or not, these were the only chemicals the company had or could get, and who would dare tell the Fascist authorities that the chemicals were defective or that the enamels could not be made. I didn't want to endanger my comrades. So, I made an enamel.

JEAN. Like a good cook who looks in the cupboard and uses whatever happens to be there, Primo went into the cellars of the company's warehouses, rummaged about, collected all the misplaced, neglected, old, decomposing chemicals he could find and concocted this weird chemical cocktail, using the deficiencies of one decaying chemical to offset the deficiencies of another defective chemical. He worked in this manner, cooking this batch and that batch until all the deficiencies working together, balanced themselves, and, the truth be told, actually enhanced each other's qualities, making a superb enamel. And how did our cook know this lucky event? He heard the right popping sounds from the bursting bubbles at the tops of the vats, smelt the right odor of fumes, saw the proper color of the chemical soup. Yes, a very ancient company secret, handed down from generation to generation. For three years, at least, and utterly unfathomable to the methodical mind of an unimaginative chemist.

(The BOY returns, he hands the mail to PRIMO.)

BOY. My mother says they shouldn't bother you with so many letters. *(The BOY exits.)*

JEAN. For an atheist, there is more faith in you than in all the believers in the world.

PRIMO *(sorting through the letters)*. If there is one, Jean, just one among all of these, isn't that reason enough?

JEAN. No. That is not enough.

PRIMO. Then you want every person to be a saint?

JEAN. I want us to look objectively at ourselves. I want us to make realistic judgments about what we can and cannot do. I want us to stop lying to ourselves. You idealists have made a catastrophe of things. Most people prefer anything to truth—their comfort, their convenience, their security, their precious self-image, their money, their power, their position in life, no matter how pathetically puny it might be. They prefer anything to truth, no matter how ugly or idiotic, anything that makes them feel good or feel "alive." *(PRIMO selects a letter, opens it, reads it.)*

Act II   AN UNCERTAIN HOUR   Page 59

WOMAN. Dear Mr. Levi, Thank you for responding to my letter. It was very kind of you to take the time to write me.

JEAN. Most people prefer anything to truth—

WOMAN. I'm trying to get our library to make your works available...

JEAN. Their comfort, their convenience, their security, their position in life, no matter how pathetically puny...

WOMAN. But, I'm not having much luck. I even offered to purchase them...

JEAN. ...anything, no matter how ugly or idiotic, anything that makes them feel good or feel "alive."

WOMAN. But, the Library Board rejected my offer.

JEAN. The enterprising, the ambitious among us, seek fame, power, and wealth.

WOMAN. They said it was best that these things be forgotten.

JEAN. No, Primo, it is not truth we seek...We don't want to know ourselves.

PRIMO. Jean, why are you doing this?

JEAN. Because he is wrong, Primo, because Dante, whom you taught me to love, the poet to whom I devoted my life, he is wrong. There is something ineffably mute at the heart of great suffering, especially the suffering that we ourselves create. We cannot remain awake in the face of so much suffering: it deadens us. Our minds, our imaginations cannot envision why we have chosen to cause so much unnecessary pain, and, what is even worse, we cannot envision a way of living that does not murder our neighbor. Our art has failed us.

PRIMO *(holding out a letter)*. This person, like you, Jean, yes, like you yourself. This person seeks the truth, and as you yourself did, this person, will find her own path. Like you, she has chosen to listen to me when I felt compelled to speak. And, I, in turn, choose now to listen to her.

(Pause.) When our century sullied the notion of truth, it also sought to destroy the idea of innocence. You were innocent, Jean, as was I. Innocent blood was shed, innocent lives have been ruined. The blood of the innocent is sacred to me, whether it be Jew or Arab, Turk or Armenian, Black or White, Gypsy or any other type of outcast. Even when it seems that words can do nothing but profane the very truth itself, nonetheless I must speak.

JEAN *(places the Army prison blanket around PRIMO).* You have based your whole life on the word, on the hope that the word will awaken us, but words themselves have fallen into a profound sleep. Yet, you continue to write in the mistaken belief that we truly desire to live together as human beings, even though the truth of our century, right to this very day, opposes you. The truth of this century negates you, Primo Levi, it negates you, your work, and your hope for us.

PRIMO. Jean, even if there is no reason, even if we live in an inferno of our own making, without any hope, we must continue. We must continue. Our dignity, our humanity demands it. If we have nothing but our love, then we must love.

JEAN *(takes one of the letters, opens it, reads it aloud).* It is my unpleasant duty to inform you that your friend Jean has taken his life according to the ancient Japanese ritual of Sepuku. In the note he left, he has asked that all his books, all his letters, all his writings be destroyed—that every sign of his existence be utterly annihilated. *(JEAN exits.)*

PRIMO *(rises, holds the Army prison blanket about him).* The night before the S.S. came for us, each took his escape from life in his own manner: some in prayer; some in drink; some in lust. Mothers prepared food for the journey.

Act II   AN UNCERTAIN HOUR   Page 61

(The BOY enters.)

BOY. What would you do? The children must eat. *(The full ENSEMBLE herds itself together, each member mumbling lullabies from their respective traditions. The WOMAN wails a "Kaddish" in the manner of a North African Jew.)*

PRIMO. The Jews of Tripoli sat in a circle, lit the ritual candles, and according to ancient custom, waited for morning, wailing lamentations. At dawn, the light of the sun fell upon us like Judas kissing his friend to betray him. The Italian guards turned their eyes away from us. Till this day I do not know whether from guilt or from shame. The S.S. Kommandant shouted *wieviel stuck.* How many pieces? How many pieces do you have for me to carry away to burn in my ovens? *(The full ENSEMBLE including PRIMO are herded onto the cattle car taking them to Auschwtiz. The sound of Christmas carols is intermixed with the sounds of the train.)* Some had managed to bring little scraps of food but it was quickly gone. Five days. Five days and nights locked in a cattle car. One bucket for a hundred people. No privacy. No water. The ceaseless rolling of the train. Trains. How many wonderful dreams and stories we have about trains, about journeys on a train. The train stopped. The guards loaded supplies for themselves for the rest of the journey. The station master watered the train while we watched through the gaps in the planks, our throats swollen with thirst. The station master had prepared a surprise Christmas feast for the S.S. guards. They started singing Christmas carols. *(A single voice beautifully and clearly sings.)*

VOICE.
> *Stille Nacht, heilige Nacht!*
> *Alles schlaeft, einsam wacht*
> *Nur das traute, hochheilige Paar*
> *Holder Knabe im lockigen Haar,*
> *Schlaf in himmlischer Ruh,*
> *Schlaf in himmlischer Ruh!*

PRIMO *(as the Christmas carol fades).* I reached my hand out to an icicle that hung down from the roof of the boxcar. A guard saw me reach. He knocked the icicle down. *(The singing stops.)*

BOY. Why?

WOMAN. How can it be
> that life goes on?
> How can it be
> that the living keep on
> living and living and living
> and the dead keep on
> dying and dying?

BOY. Is there no remembering,
> no word to be said:
> to awaken the living,
> to bury the dead?
> No one to name the new-born.
> *(The BOY sits in PRIMO's rocking chair.)*

VOICE *(from offstage).* Selekcija! *(PRIMO mimes having his face slapped.)*

PRIMO. Of all the things that I saw, of all the things that were done, whether to me or to the smallest most vulnerable, innocent child—all of these things were for me the repercussions of that single first blow, that single first slap across my left cheek, that first-felt insult to my humanity. *(PRIMO's face is slapped again. He looks at the tattoo on his left arm near his wrist.)* 174517.

BOY. This is Barbe Levi's grandmother's chair. It stands on the very spot where Barbe Levi was born. Barbe Levi loved this chair. He'd sit in it for hours and hours cleaning these old shoes, and telling me stories. Barbe Levi is dead now. They found him on the floor at the bottom of the stairs, right in front of the door to my home. My mother screamed and wouldn't let me see him. Now I have no one to bring the mail to, and no one tells me any stories. But they let me come to his room here to use the computer. They say that Barbe Levi fell down the stairwell on purpose. That he wanted to die...

VOICE *(from offstage). Selekcija! (PRIMO mimes having his face slapped.)*

BOY. ...but Barbe Levi was learning how to use the computer. He really was. He even used it to write stories for me to read. He was teaching me to write stories too. *(Pause.)* I like sitting in this chair.

PRIMO *(directly to the BOY)*. My mother and my grandmother told me many stories as they cradled me in their arms.

BOY *(carefully takes one of the old shoes, gently begins to clean it)*. Barbe Levi loved these old shoes. He never threw any of them out. Everyday he cared for them.

PRIMO *(pause)*. This is how we humans take care of each other, by the stories we tell.

BOY *(cleaning the shoes)*. For each one, he cared.

END OF PLAY

DIRECTOR'S NOTES